Flip the Flaps
Weather

Dr. Mike Goldsmith and John Butler

KINGFISHER
NEW YORK

Contents

KINGFISHER
LONDON & NEW YORK

Copyright © 2010 by Kingfisher
Published in the United States by Kingfisher,
175 Fifth Avenue, New York, NY 10010
Kingfisher is an imprint of Macmillan Children's Books, London.
All rights reserved.

Distributed in the U.S. by Macmillan,
175 Fifth Avenue, New York, NY 10010
Distributed in Canada by H.B. Fenn and Company Ltd.,
34 Nixon Road, Bolton, Ontario L7E 1W2

Library of Congress Cataloging-in-Publication Data
has been applied for.

ISBN: 978-0-7534-6442-7

Kingfisher books are available for special promotions and premiums.
For details contact: Special Markets Department,
Macmillan, 175 Fifth Avenue, New York, NY 10010

For more information, please visit www.kingfisherpublications.com

First American Edition April 2010
Printed in China
10 9 8 7 6 5 4 3 2 1
1TR/1109/TOPLF/UNTD/140MA/C

Weather words

Sunshine light from the sun

Shade a place out of the sun

Cloud tiny drops of water or ice floating in the air

Rain drops of water that fall from clouds

Lightning a flash of light in the sky

Rainbow bright colors that curve in the sky

Fog cold, damp air that is hard to see through

Hurricane a dangerous storm with very strong winds

Ice frozen water

Snow tiny pieces of ice that fall from clouds

Sunny weather

The hot, yellow sun makes daytime bright. It warms the world and makes plants grow and flowers open. When the sun makes us feel too hot, we cool off in the shade.

playing in the sunshine

flowers opening

4

1. What does the sun do?

2. Is it safe to look at the sun?

A lizard hiding in the shade

3. Is the weather colder at night?

A thirsty giraffe taking a drink

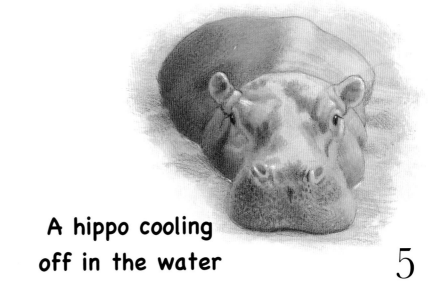

A hippo cooling off in the water

Clouds and rain

Clouds shade us from the sun, and they carry rain around the world. Rain helps plants and animals live and grow. The rain fills the rivers, which run down to the lakes and seas.

enjoying a sunny day

6

1. What are clouds made of?

2. How is rain made?

3. Do all clouds make rain?

sheltering from
sudden rain

1. Clouds are made of tiny drops of water floating in the air.

2. Sometimes the tiny drops of water in clouds stick together and grow into much bigger drops. These big drops fall as rain.

3. No. Most rain is made in thick, dark clouds.

Wet weather gear

An umbrella keeps off the rain.

A coat keeps you warm and dry.

Rubber boots keep your feet nice and dry.

7

Thunder and lightning

Sometimes the weather is stormy. Dark clouds gather and lots of rain falls. You might see lightning flash across the sky and hear the sound of thunder.

A storm begins . . .

pets keep dry inside

8

1. What is lightning?

2. Is lightning dangerous?

3. What is thunder?

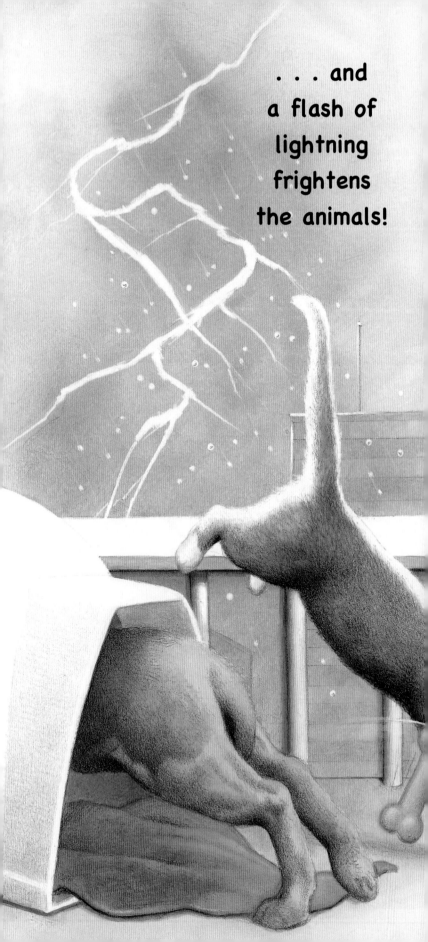

1. Lightning is a flash of light and heat in the air. It lasts for less than one second.

2. It can be, if it hits something. Tall buildings have lightning rods to send the lightning safely down to the ground.

Lightning striking the rod on a skyscraper

3. Thunder is the noise lightning makes. If nearby, it sounds like a *CRACK!* If far away, it sounds like a *R-R-RUMBLE.*

Lightning striking and damaging a tree

9

Rainbows

A rainbow is a curve of bright colors in the sky. When the rain has just stopped and the sun is shining, you often see a rainbow appear.

rain falling from thick, dark clouds

donkeys grazing on a hill

10

1. What makes
a rainbow?

2. Which colors are
in a rainbow?

3. How long do
rainbows last?

sunshine and rain make a rainbow

1. A rainbow is made when the sun shines through raindrops in the air.

2. The colors are red, orange, yellow, green, blue, indigo, and violet.

3. Most rainbows last only a few minutes. They fade away as the raindrops fall to the ground.

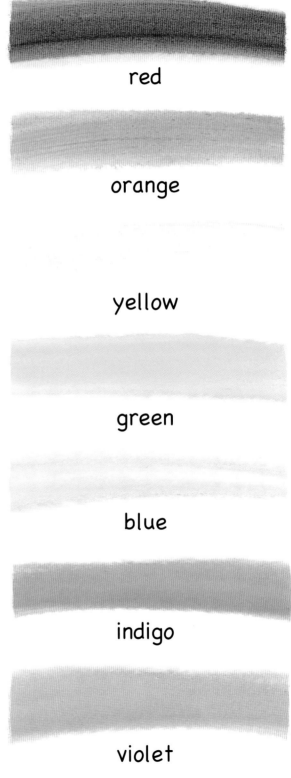

The colors of the rainbow

red

orange

yellow

green

blue

indigo

violet

11

Fog and mist

Fog is like a cloud on the ground. You cannot see far in fog, and often everything looks strange. Mist is a type of thin fog. Sometimes you can see mist and fog move and change.

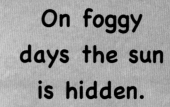

On foggy days the sun is hidden.

12

1. What is fog like?

2. When does
it get foggy?

3. Which places
are the foggiest?

When the fog
clears, the day
is sunny.

1. Fog is cold and dark. It is also damp because it is made up of water in the air.

2. It is foggy when the weather is cold and damp and no wind is blowing. Most fogs form in the winter.

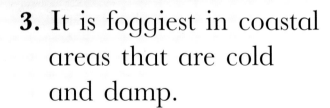

3. It is foggiest in coastal areas that are cold and damp.

Steam from hot water

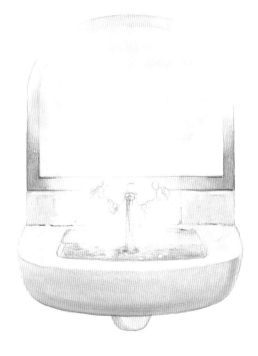

Like fog, steam is made of drops of water in the air.

13

The wind

The air is hardly ever still, and when it moves we call it the wind. If the air moves slowly, the wind is gentle, and we call it a breeze. When the wind blows hard, we call it a gale; if it is even harder, a hurricane.

The wind makes kites fly and boats sail.

14

1. What is wind?

2. Why is the wind so much stronger by the sea and on hilltops?

3. Is the wind always cold?

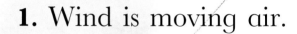

1. Wind is moving air.

2. At sea and on hills the wind is much stronger because there are no buildings in the way.

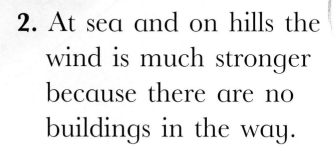

3. No, some winds can be warm or even hot. It depends on where they come from.

No wind

Breeze

Gale

Hurricane

15

Ice and snow

Sometimes it is so cold that everything is covered in white frost. Snow may fall from the clouds and lie on the ground like thick, white icing. In the coldest weather, ponds and rivers may freeze.

Usually ducks can swim in a pond.

16

1. What happens to fish in a pond when the surface freezes over?

2. What is snow?

3. What is frost?

When a
pond freezes,
the ducks walk
on top!

1. Usually there is still water underneath, and the fish are not hurt by the cold.

2. When the air is very cold, the water in clouds turns to tiny pieces of ice. These pieces flutter down as snow.

3. Frost is white ice that appears on the ground when it is freezing cold and the air is damp.

Snowflakes come in many shapes . . .

. . . some are a tidy, spiky shape.

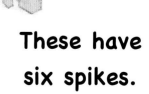

These have six spikes.

17

Index